poufs & Pillows

Accent your home with the newest home dec trend – jumbo pillows and poufs! Use super bulky and jumbo yarns, then see page 22 for smart stuffing options.

18

3

14

LEISURE ARTS, INC. • Maumelle, Arkansas

Triangles

EASY

Pillow

Finished Size: 18" (45.5 cm) square

SHOPPING LIST

Yarn (Super Bulky Weight) SUPER BULKY 6
[6 ounces, 106 yards
(170 grams, 97 meters)
per skein]:

- ☐ Brown - 2 skeins
- ☐ Green - 2 skeins
- ☐ Ecru - 2 skeins

Crochet Hook

- ☐ Size N/P (10 mm)
  or size needed for gauge

Additional Supplies

- ☐ Yarn needle
- ☐ 18" (45.5 cm) square pillow form

GAUGE INFORMATION

Each Triangle = 4¾" wide x 4¾" tall (12 cm x 12 cm)

Gauge Swatch: 4¾" wide x 4¾" tall (12 cm x 12 cm)

Work same as Triangle: 27 sc.

TRIANGLE

(Make 48 total, 16 **each** Brown, Green, and Ecru)

Ch 10.

Row 1 (Right side)**:** Sc in second ch from hook and in each ch across: 9 sc.

Note: Loop a short piece of yarn around any stitch to mark Row 1 as **right** side.

Rows 2-7: Ch 1 **(counts as first sc, now and through Row 8)**, turn; sc in next sc and in each sc across to last sc, leave last sc unworked: 3 sc.

Row 8: Ch 1, turn; sc in next sc, leave last sc unworked: 2 sc.

Edging: Ch 1, turn; sc in first 2 sc; skip first row, sc in end of next 7 rows; working in free loops of beginning ch ***(Fig. 1, page 21)***; 2 sc in first ch, sc in next 7 chs, 2 sc in next ch; sc in end of first 7 rows, skip last row; join with slip st to first sc, finish off: 27 sc.

FINISHING

Place Triangles as desired or use diagram as a guide for placement to match Triangle Floor Pillow, page 2. With **wrong** sides together and working through inside loops **only**, whipstitch Triangles together ***(Fig. 4b, page 22)***, forming 4 horizontal strips of 12 Triangles each. Whipstitch strips together in same manner, then whipstitch ends of strips together to form a tube.

Flatten tube, then whipstitch top and bottom seams, inserting pillow form before closing.

DIAGRAM

Floor Pillow

Finished Size:
28½" wide x 45½" long
x 5½" deep
(72.5 cm x 115.5 cm x 14 cm)

SHOPPING LIST

Yarn (Super Bulky Weight) SUPER BULKY 6
[6 ounces, 106 yards
(170 grams, 97 meters)
per skein]:

- ☐ Brown - 10 skeins
- ☐ Green - 7 skeins
- ☐ Ecru - 7 skeins

Crochet Hook

- ☐ Size N/P (10 mm)
  or size needed for gauge

Additional Supplies

- ☐ Yarn needle
- ☐ Safety pins (for finishing)
- ☐ 20" x 54" (51 cm x 137 cm)
  Body pillow - 2

GAUGE INFORMATION

Each Triangle = 4¾" wide x 4¾" tall
(12 cm x 12 cm);
5 sc and 5 rows = 2¼" (5.75 cm)

Gauge Swatch: 4¾" wide x 4¾" tall
(12 cm x 12 cm)

Work same as Triangle: 27 sc.

TRIANGLE

(Make 216 total, 72 **each**
Brown, Green, and Ecru)

Ch 10.

Row 1 (Right side)**:** Sc in second ch from hook and in each ch across: 9 sc.

Note: Loop a short piece of yarn around any stitch to mark Row 1 as **right** side.

Rows 2-7: Ch 1 **(counts as first sc, now and through Row 8)**, turn; sc in next sc and in each sc across to last sc, leave last sc unworked: 3 sc.

Row 8: Ch 1, turn; sc in next sc, leave last sc unworked: 2 sc.

Edging: Ch 1, turn; sc in first 2 sc; skip first row, sc in end of next 7 rows; working in free loops of beginning ch ***(Fig. 1, page 21)***; 2 sc in first ch, sc in next 7 chs, 2 sc in next ch; sc in end of first 7 rows, skip last row; join with slip st to first sc, finish off: 27 sc.

SIDE (Make 2)

With Brown, ch 12.

Row 1 (Right side)**:** Sc in second ch from hook and in each ch across: 11 sc.

Note: Mark Row 1 as **right** side.

Row 2: Ch 1, turn; sc in each sc across.

Repeat Row 2 for pattern until piece measures approximately 45½" (115.5 cm) from beginning ch, ending by working a **wrong** side row.

Edging: Ch 1, turn; 2 sc in first sc, sc in next 9 sc, 3 sc in last sc; sc evenly across ends of rows; working in free loops of beginning ch, 3 sc in first ch, sc in next 9 chs, 3 sc in next ch; sc evenly across ends of rows; join with slip st to first sc, finish off leaving a long for sewing.

FINISHING

Using diagram as a guide for placement, with **wrong** sides together, and working through inside loops **only**, whipstitch Triangles together *(Fig. 4b, page 22)*, forming 6 horizontal strips of 36 Triangles each.

Whipstitch strips together in same manner, then whipstitch ends of strips together to form a large tube.

Flatten tube. Pin one Side to one long edge of tube, centering short ends of Side to center Triangles at flattened edges and corners of Side to tips of Triangles on each side of center Triangles. Using long end, whipstitch Side to tube.

Note: To prevent the pillows from shifting inside the Floor Pillow, sew the long edges of the pillows together. See Pouf Stuffing Options on page 22 for other ideas.

Whipstitch remaining Side to opposite long edge in same manner, inserting pillows before closing.

DIAGRAM

African Flower

EASY

Pillow

Finished Size: 25½" (65 cm) from straight edge to straight edge

SHOPPING LIST

Yarn (Super Bulky Weight) SUPER BULKY 6

[5 ounces, 81 yards (142 grams, 74 meters) per skein]:

- ☐ Gold - 5 skeins
- ☐ Green - 4 skeins
- ☐ Wine - 1 skein

Crochet Hook

- ☐ Size N/P (10 mm) **or** size needed for gauge

Additional Supplies

- ☐ Yarn needle
- ☐ Sewing needle and thread
- ☐ 1 yard (1 meter) fabric for pillow form
- ☐ Polyester fiberfill

GAUGE INFORMATION

Each Motif = 8½" (21.5 cm) from straight edge to straight edge

Gauge Swatch: 3" (7.5 cm) diameter

Work same as Motif Rnd 1: 12 dc and 6 ch-1 sps.

STITCH GUIDE

LONG SINGLE CROCHET *(abbreviated LSC)*

Working **around** next ch, insert hook in ch-1 sp on Rnd 2, YO and pull up a loop even with loop on hook, YO and draw through both loops on hook.

MOTIF (Make 14)

Rnd 1 (Right side)**:** With Wine, ch 4, dc in fourth ch from hook **(3 skipped chs count as first dc)**, ch 1, (2 dc in same ch, ch 1) 5 times; join with slip st to first dc, finish off: 12 dc and 6 ch-1 sps.

Note: Loop a short piece of yarn around any stitch to mark Rnd 1 as **right** side.

Rnd 2: With **right** side facing, join Green with slip st in any ch-1 sp; ch 5 **(counts as first dc plus ch 2)**, 2 dc in same sp, ch 1, ★ (2 dc, ch 2, 2 dc) in next ch-1 sp, ch 1; repeat from ★ around, dc in same sp as first dc; join with slip st to first dc: 24 dc and 12 sps.

Rnd 3: Slip st in next ch-2 sp, ch 3 **(counts as first dc, now and throughout)**, 6 dc in same sp, ch 1, skip next ch-1 sp, ★ 7 dc in next ch-2 sp, ch 1, skip next ch-1 sp; repeat from ★ around; join with slip st to first dc, finish off: 42 dc and 6 chs.

Rnd 4: With **right** side facing, join Gold with sc in first dc of any 7-dc group ***(see Joining With Sc, page 21)***; sc in next 6 dc, work LSC, (sc in next 7 dc, work LSC) around; join with slip st to first sc: 48 sts.

Rnd 5: Ch 3, dc in next 2 sc, (dc, ch 1, dc) in next sc, dc in next 3 sc, skip next LSC, ★ dc in next 3 sc, (dc, ch 1, dc) in next sc, dc in next 3 sc, skip next LSC; repeat from ★ around; join with slip st to first dc, finish off: 48 dc and 6 ch-1 sps.

FINISHING

Using diagram as a guide for placement, with **wrong** sides together, and working through **both** loops on both pieces, whipstitch 7 Motifs together with Gold ***(Fig. 4a, page 22)***, beginning and ending in corner ch-1 sps to form front and back of Pillow.

Using one piece for a pattern and adding a ¼" (7 mm) seam allowance, cut 2 pieces of fabric for pillow form. With right sides together, sew seam, leaving a 2" (5 cm) opening for turning. Clip corners.

Turn form right side out; stuff firmly and sew opening closed.

With Gold, whipstitch front and back together in same manner, inserting pillow form before closing.

DIAGRAM

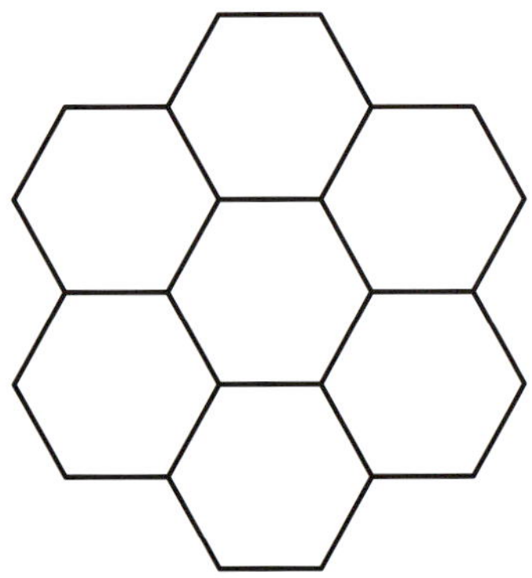

Pouf

Shown on pages 6 and 10.

Finished Size: 89" (226 cm) circumference

SHOPPING LIST

Yarn (Super Bulky Weight) SUPER BULKY 6

[5 ounces, 81 yards
(142 grams, 74 meters) per skein]:

- ☐ Gold - 7 skeins
- ☐ Green - 6 skeins
- ☐ Wine - 2 skeins

Crochet Hook

- ☐ Size N/P (10 mm) **or** size needed for gauge

Additional Supplies

- ☐ Yarn needle
- ☐ Child-size bean bag with zipper

GAUGE INFORMATION

Each Motif = 8½" (21.5 cm) from straight edge to straight edge

Each Square = 6¼" (16 cm) square

Gauge Swatch:

3" (7.5 cm) diameter

Work same as Motif Rnd 1: 12 dc and 6 ch-1 sps.

STITCH GUIDE

LONG SINGLE CROCHET *(abbreviated LSC)*

Working **around** next ch, insert hook in ch-1 sp on Rnd 2, YO and pull up a loop even with loop on hook, YO and draw through both loops on hook.

MOTIF (Make 20)

Rnd 1 (Right side)**:** With Wine, ch 4, dc in fourth ch from hook **(3 skipped chs count as first dc, now and throughout)**, ch 1, (2 dc in same ch, ch 1) 5 times; join with slip st to first dc, finish off: 12 dc and 6 ch-1 sps.

Note: Loop a short piece of yarn around any stitch to mark Rnd 1 as **right** side.

Rnd 2: With **right** side facing, join Green with slip st in any ch-1 sp, ch 5 **(counts as first dc plus ch 2, now and throughtout)**, 2 dc in same sp, ch 1, ★ (2 dc, ch 2, 2 dc) in next ch-1 sp, ch 1; repeat from ★ around, dc in same sp as first dc; join with slip st to first dc: 24 dc and 12 sps.

Rnd 3: Slip st in next ch-2 sp, ch 3 **(counts as first dc, now and throughout)**, 6 dc in same sp, ch 1, skip next ch-1 sp, ★ 7 dc in next ch-2 sp, ch 1, skip next ch-1 sp; repeat from ★ around; join with slip st to first dc, finish off: 42 dc and 6 chs.

Rnd 4: With **right** side facing, join Gold with sc in first dc of any 7-dc group ***(see Joining With Sc, page 21)***; sc in next 6 dc, work LSC, (sc in next 7 dc, work LSC) around; join with slip st to first sc: 48 sts.

Rnd 5: Ch 3, dc in next 2 sc, (dc, ch 1, dc) in next sc, dc in next 3 sc, skip next LSC, ★ dc in next 3 sc, (dc, ch 1, dc) in next sc, dc in next 3 sc, skip next LSC; repeat from ★ around; join with slip st to first dc, finish off: 48 dc and 6 ch-1 sps.

DIAGRAM

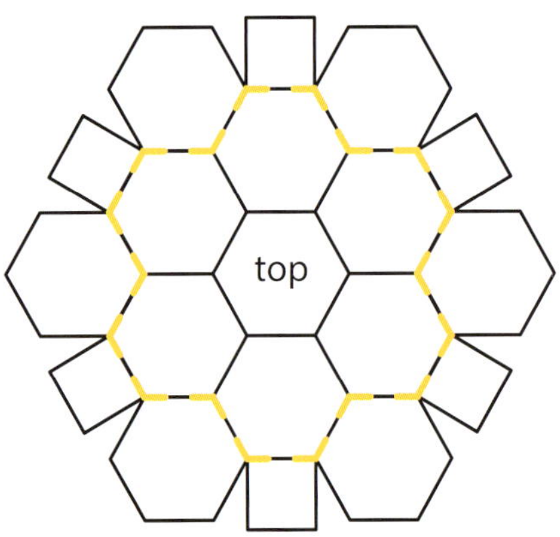

SQUARE (Make 6)

Rnd 1 (Right side)**:** With Wine, ch 4, dc in fourth ch from hook, ch 1, (2 dc in same ch, ch 1) 3 times; join with slip st to first dc, finish off: 8 dc and 4 ch-1 sps.

Note: Mark Rnd 1 as **right** side.

Rnd 2: With **right** side facing, join Green with slip st in any ch-1 sp; ch 5, 2 dc in same sp, ch 1, ★ (2 dc, ch 2, 2 dc) in next ch-1 sp, ch 1; repeat from ★ 2 times **more**, dc in same sp as first dc; join with slip st to first dc: 16 dc and 8 sps.

Rnd 3: Slip st in next ch-2 sp, ch 3, 6 dc in same sp, ch 1, skip next ch-1 sp, ★ 7 dc in next ch-2 sp, ch 1, skip next ch-1 sp; repeat from ★ 2 times **more**; join with slip st to first dc, finish off: 28 dc and 4 chs.

Rnd 4: With **right** side facing, join Gold with sc in first dc of any 7-dc group; sc in next 6 dc, work LSC, (sc in next 7 dc, work LSC) around; join with slip st to first sc: 32 sts.

Rnd 5: Ch 3, dc in next 2 sc, (dc, ch 1, dc) in next sc, dc in next 3 sc, skip next LSC, ★ dc in next 3 sc, (dc, ch 1, dc) in next sc, dc in next 3 sc, skip next LSC; repeat from ★ 2 times **more**; join with slip st to first dc, finish off: 32 dc and 4 ch-1 sps.

FINISHING

Using diagram as a guide for placement, with **wrong** sides together, and working through **both** loops on both pieces, whipstitch 7 Motifs together with Gold ***(Fig. 4a, page 22)***, beginning and ending in corner ch-1 sps to form center of top. Whipstitch 6 Motifs and 6 Squares to top in same manner. Whipstitch remaining 7 Motifs together to form bottom, then join top to bottom in same manner, inserting bean bag before closing.

Note: Remove the stuffing from the bean bag as needed in order to insert it into the Pouf, then replace the stuffing until desired fullness is achieved. See Pouf Stuffing Options on page 22 for other ideas.

Post Stitch

EASY

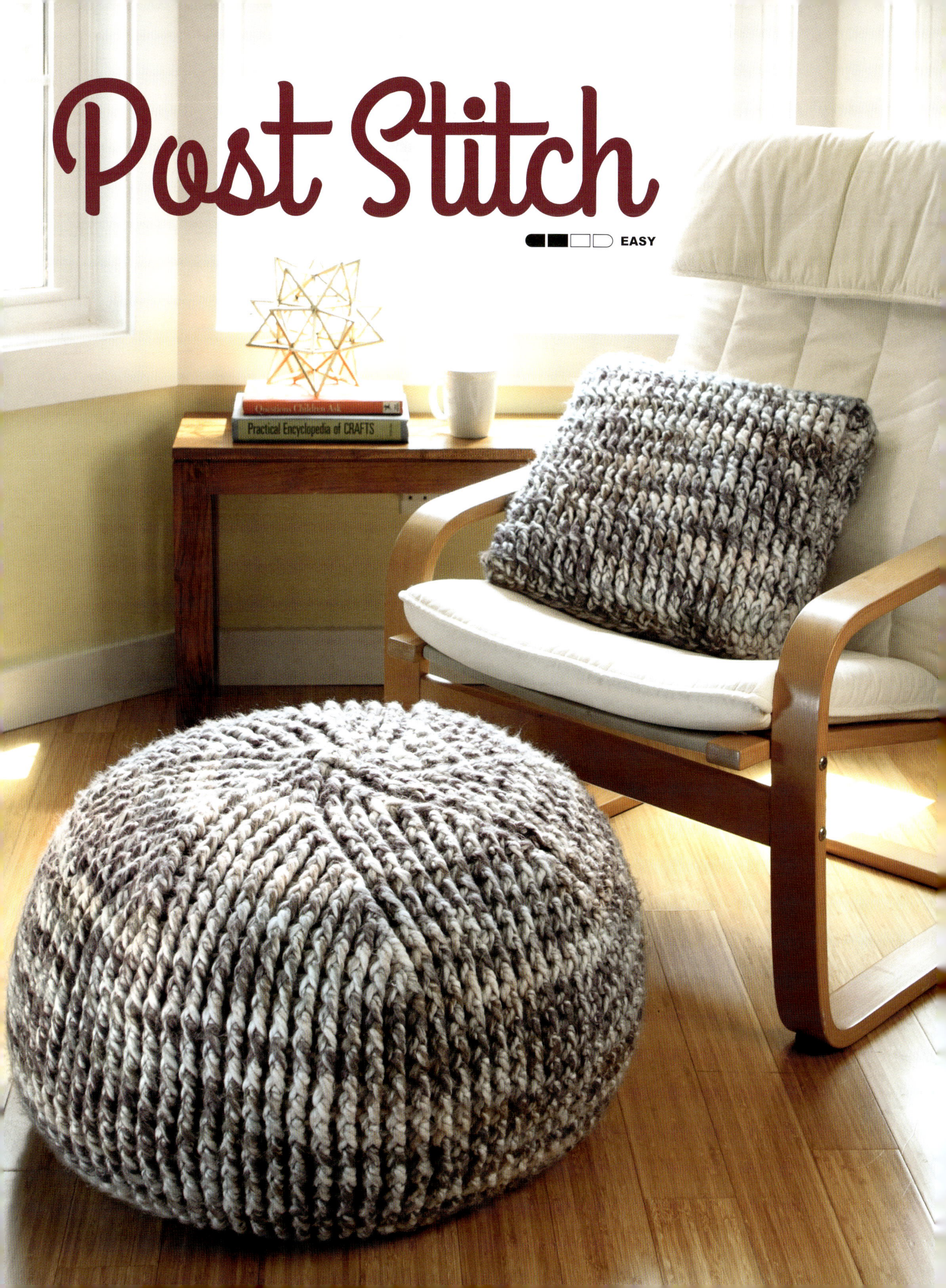

Pillow

Shown on pages 11 and 13.

Finished Size: 18" (45.5 cm) square

SHOPPING LIST

Yarn (Jumbo Weight) JUMBO 7

[3.5 ounces, 55 yards
(100 grams, 50 meters) per skein]:

- ☐ 5 skeins

Crochet Hook

- ☐ Size N/P (10 mm)
  or size needed for gauge

Additional Supplies

- ☐ Yarn needle
- ☐ 18" (45.5 cm) square pillow form

GAUGE INFORMATION

In Front pattern, 6 sts = 4" (10 cm);
3 rows = 3" (7.5 cm)

In Back pattern, 6 dc and 3 rows = 5" (12.75 cm)

Gauge Swatch: 5" (12.75) square

Foundation Row: Ch 4, YO, insert hook in fourth ch from hook **(3 skipped chs count as first dc)**, YO and pull up a loop (3 loops on hook), YO and draw through one loop on hook **(ch made)**, (YO and draw through 2 loops on hook) twice **(first Fdc made)**, work Fdc for a total of 6 sts.

Rows 1 and 2: Ch 3 **(counts as first dc)**, turn; dc in next st and in each st across.

Finish off.

STITCH GUIDE

FOUNDATION DOUBLE CROCHET
(abbreviated Fdc)

YO, insert hook in ch at base of previous Fdc ***(Fig. 3, page 22)***, YO and pull up a loop (3 loops on hook), YO and draw through one loop on hook **(ch made)**, (YO and draw through 2 loops on hook) twice **(Fdc made)**.

FRONT POST DOUBLE CROCHET
(abbreviated FPdc)

YO, insert hook from **front** to **back** around post of st indicated ***(Fig. 2, page 21)***, YO and pull up a loop (3 loops on hook), (YO and draw through 2 loops on hook) twice

BACK POST DOUBLE CROCHET
(abbreviated BPdc)

YO, insert hook from **back** to **front** around post of st indicated ***(Fig. 2, page 21)***, YO and pull up a loop (3 loops on hook), (YO and draw through 2 loops on hook) twice.

FRONT

Foundation Row (Right side)**:** Ch 4, YO, insert hook in fourth ch from hook (**3 skipped chs count as first dc**), YO and pull up a loop (3 loops on hook), YO and draw through one loop on hook (**ch made**), (YO and draw through 2 loops on hook) twice (**first Fdc made**), work Fdc for a total of 26 sts.

Note: Loop a short piece of yarn around any stitch to mark Foundation Row as **right** side and **bottom** edge.

Row 1: Ch 3 (**counts as first dc, now and throughout**), turn; work BPdc around next Fdc and each Fdc across to last dc, dc in last dc.

Row 2: Ch 3, turn; work FPdc around next st and each st across to last dc, dc in last dc.

Row 3: Ch 3, turn; work BPdc around next st and each st across to last dc, dc in last dc.

Rows 4-17: Repeat Rows 2 and 3, 7 times.

Finish off.

BACK

Foundation Row (Right side)**:** Ch 4, YO, insert hook in fourth ch from hook (**3 skipped chs count as first dc**), YO and pull up a loop (3 loops on hook), YO and draw through one loop on hook (**ch made**), (YO and draw through 2 loops on hook) twice (**first Fdc made**), work Fdc for a total of 21 sts.

Note: Mark Foundation Row as **right** side and **bottom** edge.

Rows 1-10: Ch 3, turn; dc in next st and in each st across.

Finish off leaving a long end for sewing.

With **wrong** sides and bottom edges together, sew Front and Back together, inserting pillow form before closing.

Pouf

Shown on pages 11 and 15.

Finished Size:
56" (142 cm) circumference

SHOPPING LIST

Yarn (Jumbo Weight) JUMBO 7
[3.5 ounces, 55 yards
(100 grams, 50 meters)
per skein]:
☐ 19 skeins

Crochet Hook
☐ Size N/P (10 mm)
or size needed for gauge

Additional Supplies
☐ Child-size bean bag
with zipper

GAUGE INFORMATION

6 FPdc = 4" (10 cm)

Gauge Swatch:
7" (17.75 cm) diameter
Work same as Body through Rnd 3: 21 FPdc.

STITCH GUIDE

FRONT POST DOUBLE CROCHET
(abbreviated FPdc)
YO, insert hook from **front** to **back** around post of st indicated ***(Fig. 2, page 21)***, YO and pull up a loop (3 loops on hook), (YO and draw through 2 loops on hook) twice.

FRONT POST DOUBLE CROCHET 2 TOGETHER
(abbreviated FPdc2tog)
(uses next 2 FPdc)
★ YO, insert hook from **front** to **back** around post of **next** FPdc ***(Fig. 2, page 21)***, YO and pull up a loop, YO and draw through 2 loops on hook; repeat from ★ once **more**, YO and draw through all 3 loops on hook **(counts as one FPdc)**.

SINGLE CROCHET 2 TOGETHER
(abbreviated sc2tog)
Pull up a loop in each of next 2 FPdc, YO and draw through all 3 loops on hook **(counts as one sc)**.

BODY

Ch 4; join with slip st to form a ring.

Rnd 1 (Right side)**:** Ch 1, 7 sc in ring; do **not** join, place marker to indicate beginning of rnd ***(see Markers, page 21)***.

Rnd 2: 2 Dc in each sc around: 14 dc.

Rnd 3: ★ Work 2 FPdc around next dc, work FPdc around next dc; repeat from ★ around: 21 FPdc.

Rnd 4: ★ Work 2 FPdc around next FPdc, work FPdc around each of next 2 FPdc; repeat from ★ around: 28 FPdc.

Rnd 5: ★ Work 2 FPdc around next FPdc, work FPdc around each of next 3 FPdc; repeat from ★ around: 35 FPdc.

Rnd 6: ★ Work 2 FPdc around next FPdc, work FPdc around each of next 4 FPdc; repeat from ★ around: 42 FPdc.

Rnd 7: ★ Work 2 FPdc around next FPdc, work FPdc around each of next 5 FPdc; repeat from ★ around: 49 FPdc.

Rnd 8: ★ Work 2 FPdc around next FPdc, work FPdc around each of next 6 FPdc; repeat from ★ around: 56 FPdc.

Rnd 9: ★ Work 2 FPdc around next FPdc, work FPdc around each of next 7 FPdc; repeat from ★ around: 63 FPdc.

Rnd 10: ★ Work 2 FPdc around next FPdc, work FPdc around each of next 8 FPdc; repeat from ★ around: 70 FPdc.

Rnd 11: ★ Work 2 FPdc around next FPdc, work FPdc around each of next 9 FPdc; repeat from ★ around: 77 FPdc.

Rnd 12: ★ Work 2 FPdc around next FPdc, work FPdc around each of next 10 FPdc; repeat from ★ around: 84 FPdc.

Rnds 13-27: Work FPdc around each FPdc around.

Rnd 28: ★ Work FPdc2tog, work FPdc around each of next 10 FPdc; repeat from ★ around: 77 FPdc.

Rnd 29: ★ Work FPdc2tog, work FPdc around each of next 9 FPdc; repeat from ★ around: 70 FPdc.

Rnd 30: ★ Work FPdc2tog, work FPdc around each of next 8 FPdc; repeat from ★ around: 63 FPdc.

Rnd 31: ★ Work FPdc2tog, work FPdc around each of next 7 FPdc; repeat from ★ around: 56 FPdc.

Rnd 32: ★ Work FPdc2tog, work FPdc around each of next 6 FPdc; repeat from ★ around: 49 FPdc.

Rnd 33: ★ Work FPdc2tog, work FPdc around each of next 5 FPdc; repeat from ★ around: 42 FPdc.

Rnd 34: ★ Work FPdc2tog, work FPdc around each of next 4 FPdc; repeat from ★ around: 35 FPdc.

Remove the stuffing from bean bag as needed to insert into Pouf, then replace the stuffing until desired fullness is achieved. See Pouf Stuffing Options on page 22 for other ideas.

Rnd 35: ★ Work FPdc2tog, work FPdc around each of next 3 FPdc; repeat from ★ around: 28 FPdc.

Rnd 36: ★ Work FPdc2tog, work FPdc around each of next 2 FPdc; repeat from ★ around: 21 FPdc.

Rnd 37: ★ Work FPdc2tog, work FPdc around next FPdc; repeat from ★ around: 14 FPdc.

Rnd 38: Work FPdc2tog around: 7 FPdc.

Rnd 39: Sc2tog 3 times, sc in next FPdc; slip st in next sc; finish off: 4 sc.

Columns

EASY

Pillow

Finished Size: 18" (45.5 cm) square

SHOPPING LIST

Yarn (Jumbo Weight) JUMBO 7
[3.5 ounces, 55 yards (100 grams, 50 meters) per skein]:
- ☐ 5 skeins

Crochet Hook
- ☐ Size N/P (10 mm) **or** size needed for gauge

Additional Supplies
- ☐ Yarn needle
- ☐ 18" (45.5 cm) square pillow form

STITCH GUIDE

FOUNDATION DOUBLE CROCHET ***(abbreviated Fdc)***

YO, insert hook in ch at base of previous Fdc ***(Fig. 3, page 22)***, YO and pull up a loop (3 loops on hook), YO and draw through one loop on hook **(ch made)**, (YO and draw through 2 loops on hook) twice **(Fdc made)**.

FRONT POST DOUBLE CROCHET ***(abbreviated FPdc)***

YO, insert hook from **front** to **back** around post of st indicated ***(Fig. 2, page 21)***, YO and pull up a loop (3 loops on hook), (YO and draw through 2 loops on hook) twice.

BACK POST DOUBLE CROCHET ***(abbreviated BPdc)***

YO, insert hook from **back** to **front** around post of st indicated ***(Fig. 2, page 21)***, YO and pull up a loop (3 loops on hook), (YO and draw through 2 loops on hook) twice.

GAUGE INFORMATION

In pattern, 4 sts = 3" (7.5 cm); 3 rows = 4½" (11.5 cm)

Gauge Swatch: 3" wide x 4½" high (7.5 cm x 11.5 cm)

Foundation Row: Ch 4, YO, insert hook in fourth ch from hook **(3 skipped chs count as first dc)**, YO and pull up a loop (3 loops on hook), YO and draw through one loop on hook **(ch made)**, (YO and draw through 2 loops on hook) twice **(first Fdc made)**, work Fdc for a total of 4 sts.

Rows 1 and 2: Ch 3 **(counts as first dc)**, turn; dc in next st and in each st across.

Finish off.

FRONT

Foundation Row (Right side)**:** Ch 4, YO, insert hook in fourth ch from hook **(3 skipped chs count as first dc)**, YO and pull up a loop (3 loops on hook), YO and draw through one loop on hook **(ch made)**, (YO and draw through 2 loops on hook) twice **(first Fdc made)**, work Fdc for a total of 24 sts.

Note: Loop a short piece of yarn around any stitch to mark Foundation Row as **right** side and **bottom** edge.

Row 1: Ch 3 **(counts as first dc, now and throughout)**, turn; dc in next 3 Fdc, (work BPdc around next Fdc, dc in next 4 Fdc) across.

Row 2: Ch 3, turn; dc in next 3 dc, (work FPdc around next st, dc in next 4 dc) across.

Row 3: Ch 3, turn; dc in next 3 dc, (work BPdc around next st, dc in next 4 dc) across.

Rows 4-11: Repeat Rows 2 and 3, 4 times.

Finish off leaving a long end for sewing.

BACK

Foundation Row

(Right side)**:** Ch 4, YO, insert hook in fourth ch from hook **(3 skipped chs count as first dc)**, YO and pull up a loop (3 loops on hook), YO and draw through one loop on hook **(ch made)**, (YO and draw through 2 loops on hook) twice **(first Fdc made)**, work Fdc for a total of 24 sts.

Note: Mark Foundation Row as **right** side and **bottom** edge.

Row 1: Ch 3, turn; dc in next st and in each st across.

Rows 2-11: Ch 3, turn; dc in next dc and in each dc across.

Finish off.

With **wrong** sides and bottom edges together, sew Back and Front together, inserting pillow form before closing.

Pouf

Shown on page 16 and 19.

Finished Size: 24" (61 cm) square

SHOPPING LIST

Yarn (Jumbo Weight)

[3.5 ounces, 55 yards (100 grams, 50 meters) per skein]:

- ☐ 17 skeins

Crochet Hook

- ☐ Size Q (16 mm) **or** size needed for gauge

Additional Supplies

- ☐ Yarn needle
- ☐ Inflatable ottoman
- ☐ Foam padding or batting

GAUGE INFORMATION

In pattern, 4 sts = 4" (10 cm);
4 rows = 6" (15.25 cm)

Gauge Swatch: 4" wide x 6" high (10 cm x 15.25 cm)

Foundation Row: Ch 4, YO, insert hook in fourth ch from hook **(3 skipped chs count as first dc)**, YO and pull up a loop (3 loops on hook), YO and draw through one loop on hook **(ch made)**, (YO and draw through 2 loops on hook) twice **(first Fdc made)**, work Fdc for a total of 4 sts.

Rows 1-3: Ch 3 **(counts as first dc)**, turn; dc in next st and in each st across.

Finish off.

STITCH GUIDE

FOUNDATION DOUBLE CROCHET ***(abbreviated Fdc)***

YO, insert hook in ch at base of previous Fdc ***(Fig. 3, page 22)***, YO and pull up a loop (3 loops on hook), YO and draw through one loop on hook **(ch made)**, (YO and draw through 2 loops on hook) twice **(Fdc made)**.

FRONT POST DOUBLE CROCHET ***(abbreviated FPdc)***

YO, insert hook from **front** to **back** around post of st indicated ***(Fig. 2, page 21)***, YO and pull up a loop (3 loops on hook), (YO and draw through 2 loops on hook) twice.

BACK POST DOUBLE CROCHET ***(abbreviated BPdc)***

YO, insert hook from **back** to **front** around post of st indicated ***(Fig. 2, page 21)***, YO and pull up a loop (3 loops on hook), (YO and draw through 2 loops on hook) twice.

BASE (Make 2)

Foundation Row (Right side)**:** Ch 4, YO, insert hook in fourth ch from hook **(3 skipped chs count as first dc)**, YO and pull up a loop (3 loops on hook), YO and draw through one loop on hook **(ch made)**, (YO and draw through 2 loops on hook) twice **(first Fdc made)**, work Fdc for a total of 24 sts.

Note: Loop a short piece of yarn around any stitch to mark Foundation Row as **right** side.

Rows 1-15: Ch 3 **(counts as first dc, now and throughout)**, turn; dc in next st and in each st across.

Finish off.

SIDE (Make 4)

Foundation Row (Right side)**:** Ch 4, YO, insert hook in fourth ch from hook **(3 skipped chs count as first dc)**, YO and pull up a loop (3 loops on hook), YO and draw through one loop on hook **(ch made)**, (YO and draw through 2 loops on hook) twice **(first Fdc made)**, work Fdc for a total of 24 sts.

Note: Mark Foundation Row as **right** side and **bottom** edge.

Row 1: Ch 3, turn; dc in next 3 Fdc, work BPdc around next Fdc, (dc in next 4 Fdc, work BPdc around next Fdc) across to last 4 sts, dc in last 4 sts.

Row 2: Ch 3, turn; dc in next 3 dc, work FPdc around next st, (dc in next 4 dc, work FPdc around next st) across to last 4 dc, dc in last 4 dc.

Row 3: Ch 3, turn; dc in next 3 dc, work BPdc around next st, (dc in next 4 dc, work BPdc around next st) across to last 4 dc, dc in last 4 dc.

Rows 4-15: Repeat Rows 2 and 3, 6 times.

Finish off.

FINISHING

With **wrong** sides and bottom edges together, sew ends of rows of Sides together to form a large cube.

Sew one Base to sts at top edge of Sides.

Sew remaining Base to bottom edges of Sides, inserting stuffing before closing ***(see note below)***.

Note: We used an inflatable ottoman cube covered with 5 pieces of 1" (2.5 cm) thick foam padding, placing the valve at the bottom of the crocheted cube without any padding so that it would be accessible for re-inflating. See Pouf Stuffing Options on page 22 for other ideas.

General Instructions

ABBREVIATIONS

BPdc	Back Post double crochet(s)
ch(s)	chain(s)
cm	centimeters
dc	double crochet(s)
Fdc	Foundation double crochet(s)
FPdc	Front Post double crochet(s)
FPdc2tog	Front Post double crochet 2 together
LSC	long single crochet(s)
mm	millimeters
Rnd(s)	Round(s)
sc	single crochet(s)
sc2tog	single crochet 2 together
sp(s)	space(s)
st(s)	stitch(es)
YO	yarn over

SYMBOLS & TERMS

★ — work instructions following ★ as many **more** times as indicated in addition to the first time.

( ) or **[ ]** — work enclosed instructions **as many** times as specified by the number immediately following **or** work all enclosed instructions in the stitch or space indicated **or** contains explanatory remarks.

colon (:) — the number(s) given after a colon at the end of a row or round denote(s) the number of stitches or spaces you should have on that row or round.

GAUGE

Exact gauge is **essential** for proper size. Before beginning your project, make the sample swatch given in the individual instructions in the yarn and hook specified. After completing the swatch, measure it, counting your stitches and rows or rounds carefully. If your swatch is larger or smaller than specified, **make another, changing hook size to get the correct gauge**. Keep trying until you find the size hook that will give you the specified gauge.

Yarn Weight Symbol & Names	LACE 0	SUPER FINE 1	FINE 2	LIGHT 3	MEDIUM 4	BULKY 5	SUPER BULKY 6	JUMBO 7
Type of Yarns in Category	Fingering, size 10 crochet thread	Sock, Fingering, Baby	Sport, Baby	DK, Light Worsted	Worsted, Afghan, Aran	Chunky, Craft, Rug	Super Bulky, Roving	Jumbo, Roving
Crochet Gauge* Ranges in Single Crochet to 4" (10 cm)	32-42 sts**	21-32 sts	16-20 sts	12-17 sts	11-14 sts	8-11 sts	6-9 sts	5 sts and fewer
Advised Hook Size Range	Steel*** 6 to 8, Regular hook B-1	B-1 to E-4	E-4 to 7	7 to I-9	I-9 to K-10½	K-10½ to M/N-13	M/N-13 to Q	Q and larger

*GUIDELINES ONLY: The chart above reflects the most commonly used gauges and hook sizes for specific yarn categories.

** Lace weight yarns are usually crocheted with larger hooks to create lacy openwork patterns. Accordingly, a gauge range is difficult to determine. Always follow the gauge stated in your pattern.

*** Steel crochet hooks are sized differently from regular hooks–the higher the number, the smaller the hook, which is the reverse of regular hook sizing.

MARKERS

Markers are used to help distinguish the beginning of each round being worked. Place a 2" (5 cm) piece of yarn before the first stitch of each round, moving the marker after each round is complete.

JOINING WITH SC

When instructed to join with sc, begin with a slip knot on hook. Insert hook in stitch or space indicated, YO and pull up a loop, YO and draw through both loops on hook.

FREE LOOPS OF A CHAIN

When instructed to work in free loops of a chain, work in loop indicated by arrow ***(Fig. 1)***.

Fig. 1

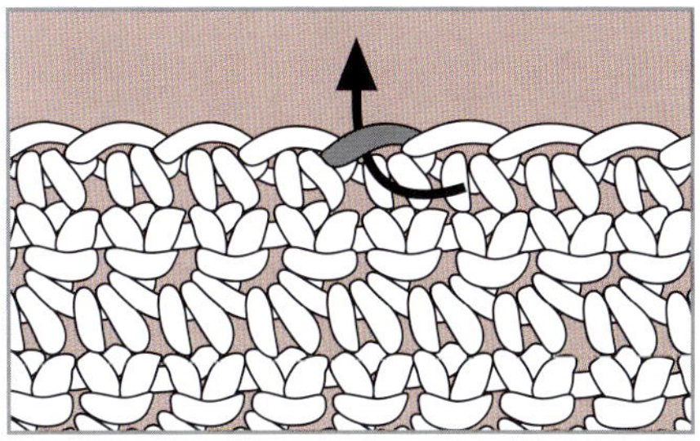

POST STITCH

Work around post of stitch indicated, inserting hook in direction of arrow ***(Fig. 2)***.

Fig. 2

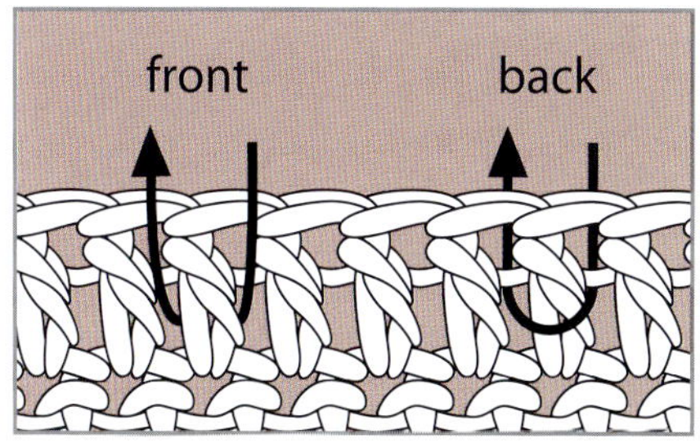

CROCHET TERMINOLOGY		
UNITED STATES		INTERNATIONAL
slip stitch (slip st)	=	single crochet (sc)
single crochet (sc)	=	double crochet (dc)
half double crochet (hdc)	=	half treble crochet (htr)
double crochet (dc)	=	treble crochet (tr)
treble crochet (tr)	=	double treble crochet (dtr)
double treble crochet (dtr)	=	triple treble crochet (ttr)
triple treble crochet (tr tr)	=	quadruple treble crochet (qtr)
skip	=	miss

CROCHET HOOKS																	
U.S.	B-1	C-2	D-3	E-4	F-5	G-6	7	H-8	I-9	J-10	K-10½	L-11	M/N-13	N/P-15	P/Q	Q	S
Metric - mm	2.25	2.75	3.25	3.5	3.75	4	4.5	5	5.5	6	6.5	8	9	10	15	16	19

BEGINNER	Projects for first-time crocheters using basic stitches. Minimal shaping.
EASY	Projects using yarn with basic stitches, repetitive stitch patterns, simple color changes, and simple shaping and finishing.
INTERMEDIATE	Projects using a variety of techniques, such as basic lace patterns or color patterns, mid-level shaping and finishing.
EXPERIENCED	Projects with intricate stitch patterns, techniques and dimension, such as non-repeating patterns, multi-color techniques, fine threads, small hooks, detailed shaping and refined finishing.

FOUNDATION DOUBLE CROCHET

(abbreviated Fdc)

YO, insert hook in ch at base of previous Fdc ***(Fig. 3)***, YO and pull up a loop (3 loops on hook), YO and draw through one loop on hook (**ch made**), (YO and draw through 2 loops on hook) twice (**Fdc made**).

Fig. 3

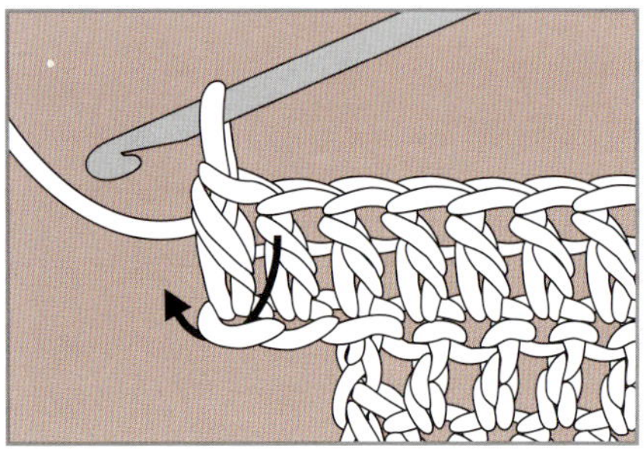

WHIPSTITCH

With **wrong** sides together, sew through **both** pieces once to secure the beginning of the seam, leaving an ample yarn end to weave in later. Working through **both** loops of each stitch on **both** pieces ***(Fig. 4a)*** **or** through inside loops only on **both** pieces ***(Fig. 4b)***, insert the needle from **front** to **back** and pull yarn through. ★ Bring the needle around and insert it from **front** to **back** through next stitch and pull yarn through; repeat from ★ across.

Fig. 4a

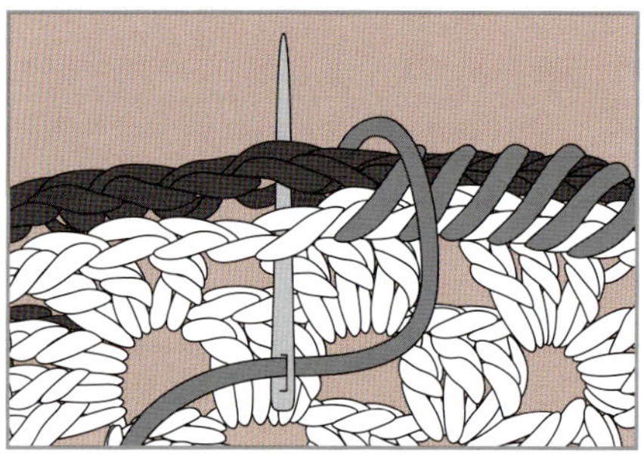

Fig. 4b

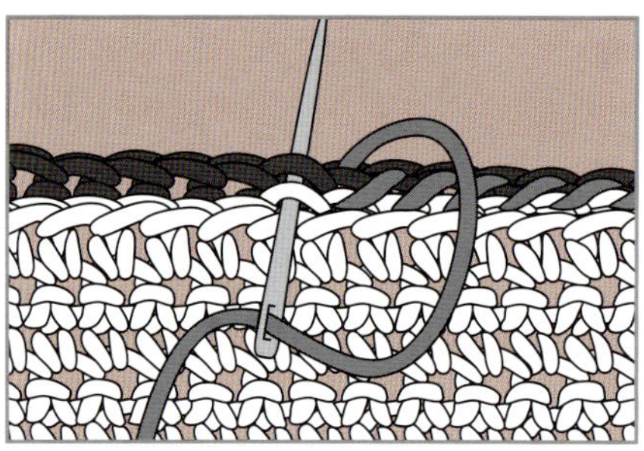

POUF STUFFING OPTIONS

There are many options available for stuffing your poufs. If you want to avoid the expense of stuffing them with all new pads or pillows, or if you simply enjoy recycling, consider using clean old towels, sheets, blankets, clothing, or other large pieces of fabric. Any resulting lumps in the stuffing can be smoothed out by adding bits of polyester fiberfill or wrapping the mass in batting until the desired size and look is achieved.

Meet The Designer: Ashley Leither

Ashley Leither dabbled in crochet and knitting during high school, but her crochet obsession didn't start until about 10 years later.

"My youngest daughter received a crochet hat as a gift when she was about 18 months old, and I thought it was so beautiful that I wanted to learn to crochet," she said. "So I went to the craft store, bought a learn-to-crochet kit and some pretty yarn, and learned to crochet the basics. I couldn't put my hooks down! There weren't enough hours in the day to crochet everything I had on my wish list. I then started coming up with ideas of things I wanted to make and started writing my own patterns."

Since then, Ashley has created more than 100 designs, with beanies and blankets being her favorite projects.

"I am a stay-at-home mom to two beautiful little girls, who keep me busy and who are my inspiration for designing," she said. "Yarn is my life, but when I am not playing with my yarn, my family and I love to go bowling, watch movies, explore new places, and attend car shows. As long as we are together, we are having fun!"

More of Ashley's designs may be found in the Leisure Arts book, *Little Animals Headgear* (#6642). She also is active on social media and has a website, AshleyDesignsCorner.com.

Yarn Information

Items in this book were made using either Super Bulky or Jumbo weight yarn. Any brand of of the specified weight of yarn may be used. It is best to refer to the yardage/meters when determining how many balls or skeins to purchase. Remember, to arrive at the finished size, it is the GAUGE/TENSION that is important, not the brand of yarn.

For your convenience, listed below are the specific yarns used to create our photography models. Because yarn manufacturers make frequent changes in their product lines, you may sometimes find it necessary to use a substitute yarn or to search for the discontinued product at alternate suppliers (locally or online).

TRIANGLES PILLOW
Lion Brand® Wool-Ease® Thick & Quick®
Brown - #122 Taupe
Green - #178 Cilantro
Ecru - #123 Oatmeal

TRIANGLES FLOOR PILLOW
Lion Brand® Wool-Ease® Thick & Quick®
Brown - #122 Taupe
Green - #178 Cilantro
Ecru - #123 Oatmeal

AFRICAN FLOWER PILLOW
Lion Brand® Hometown USA®
Gold - #170 Las Vegas Gold
Green - #175 Montpelier Peacock
Wine - #189 Napa Valley Pinot

AFRICAN FLOWER POUF
Lion Brand® Hometown USA®
Gold - #170 Las Vegas Gold
Green - #175 Montpelier Peacock
Wine - #189 Napa Valley Pinot

POST STITCH PILLOW
Lion Brand® Color Clouds®
#204 Thunder

POST STITCH POUF
Lion Brand® Color Clouds®
#204 Thunder

COLUMNS PILLOW
Lion Brand® Color Clouds®
#205 Ice Storm

COLUMNS POUF
Lion Brand® Color Clouds®
#205 Ice Storm

We have made every effort to ensure that these instructions are accurate and complete. We cannot, however, be responsible for human error, typographical mistakes, or variations in individual work.

Production Team: Instructional/Technical Editor - Sarah J. Green; Editorial Writer - Susan Frantz Wiles; Senior Graphic Artist - Lora Puls; Graphic Artist - Kellie McAnulty; Photo Stylist - Lori Wenger; and Photographer - Jason Masters.